This is the
HISTORY
of the

_____

FAMILY

OUR FAMILY HISTORY

Introduction by Neil Grant

MALLARD PRESS

ACKNOWLEDGEMENTS

The publishers would like to thank the following for their permission to reproduce the photographic material:

Bridgeman Art Library/The Museums at Stony Brook, New York 7 left; Culver Pictures Inc. 3 right, 5; Dover Publications Inc. 14, 18, 20, 24, 28, 32, 64, 66, 72, 76, 82, 86, 90, 92, 94, 98, 104, 106, 110, 114, 116-118; Jeanne Dubi 15; E.T. Archive 7 right; Mary Evans Picture Library front of slipcase top and centre right, 6, 12; Robert Harding Picture Library 11; Hulton-Deutsch/Bettmann Archive Inc. 4; Octopus Group Ltd/British Library 16/Public Record Office, Controller of Her Majesty's Stationery Office (Crown copyright record) front of slipcase centre left, 13/F.G. Tyack 2-3/John Webb front of slipcase bottom; Judith Schecter 9.

An Imprint of BDD Promotional Book Company, Inc.
666 Fifth Avenue, New York, N.Y. 10103

"Mallard Press and its accompanying design and logo are trademarks of BDD Promotional Book Company, Inc."

Copyright © The Hamlyn Publishing Group Limited 1990

First published in the United States of America in 1990 by The Mallard Press

ISBN 0792-45286-0

Produced by Mandarin Offset
Printed in Hong Kong

Introduction

Tracing your ancestors and creating your own family tree can be a fascinating pastime and great fun too, particularly if your forebears lived in other countries, you suspect you may be the long lost chief of a Scottish clan or feel you can claim descent from some famous personality.

Although you probably know the names and addresses of your immediate forebears, the chances are that you may have lost track of many of your relatives, simply because families don't stay put – they expand and move on to new places. Most people have childhood memories of overhearing stories about other members of the family. Such tales and recollections often contain a wealth of colorful detail and may vary with each telling. It is possible

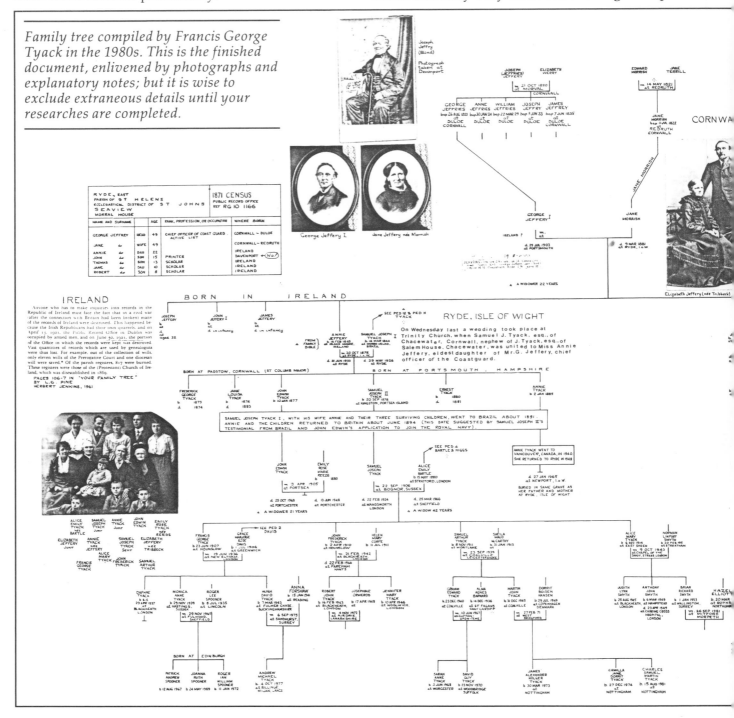

Family tree compiled by Francis George Tyack in the 1980s. This is the finished document, enlivened by photographs and explanatory notes; but it is wise to exclude extraneous details until your researches are completed.

too, that the reason why Great Aunt Martha disinherited cousin Herman and refused to let him darken the family threshold ever again, remains something of an enigma. Such stories are frequently recounted at family gatherings but this kind of fascinating information can so easily be lost or forgotten if relatives drift apart. Fortunately, most families have one loyal member who keeps in touch with everyone else, including cousins in far flung places.

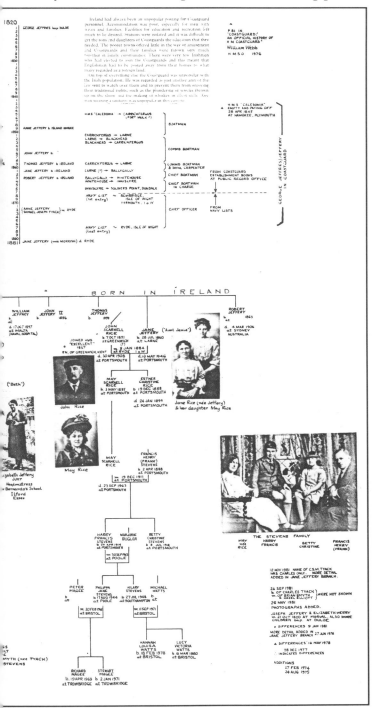

Immigrants moving west on the Canadian Pacific Railway, about 100 years ago. Pursuing your family history will probably take you to distant places, and much of your research will be conducted by mail.

Our Family History enables you to build up a detailed picture of your ancestral line. To get you started, the first section contains practical advice on how to conduct your research, including a list of useful addresses and suggestions for further reading.

The second section is for you to complete. The idea is to create in these pages a personal record book of your very own family history – a unique album to treasure and even pass down to your own children and grandchildren. Here you will find the framework of a family tree to be filled in according to the information you have gathered about your forebears, as well as key headings for setting out basic details, which may be enhanced with documents and photographs of people, places and events.

The Family Tree

The first step in tracing your family history is to complete the family tree as far as you can. A family tree looks like an inverted pyramid. The researcher or genealogist is the point at the bottom. The next generation contains two people – the parents. The next generation four, the next eight, and so on. After eight generations, the number of direct ancestors rises to 256 – assuming there has been no intermarriage between cousins! You will soon discover that it is impracticable to pursue *all* your ancestors for more than four or five generations. However, it is up to you to decide which line you want to follow.

Genealogy is usually concerned with descent through the male line – father, father's father, etc. – but unless you are trying to prove that you are the heir to, say, a vacant earldom there is no particular reason why you should follow this patriarchal trail. Moreover, once you have decided to follow a particular ancestral line, you should not be too single-minded about it. Any information you discover about other relatives should be recorded, for that branch of the family may become interesting or even more relevant at a later stage.

Which branch you pursue may well be decided for you by availability – or non-availability – of facts. Descendants of American immigrants, having established the identity of their immigrant forebears, will have to pursue the search in another country, and much of their success will depend on the country and the social class of their ancestors. If, for example, your ancestors arrived as slaves from Africa, you will not find any documentary evidence

A poor family photographed in front of their Louisiana cabin at the beginning of this century. Besides their intrinsic fascination, old photographs can sometimes provide unexpected clues.

before that time, although, as the example of *Roots* showed, oral evidence can be very productive. If your ancestors were, say, English, you will stand a greater chance of success if the immigrant was the son of a landed family rather than an indentured servant. However, there are always exceptions.

It is best not to be too ambitious in pursuit of distant ancestors for a great deal depends on luck, and on the amount of time and effort you are able and prepared to put into the search. It is impossible to judge how far back you can expect to go except in very broad terms, but in general there is a fair chance of tracing your ancestors back to 1800 or a little earlier. Beyond that, documentary evidence is more scarce and luck plays an increasing part. In some countries, including the United States and England, documentary records are better preserved than they are in others, thanks to relative freedom from major social upheavals. In a country like Poland or Russia, the situation is less satisfactory, and there are additional problems such as the language barrier or possible changes of family name to consider, though given time and effort none of these problems is necessarily insurmountable.

Although documentary records become increasingly patchy before the 19th century, there are some compensations. Populations, besides being much smaller, were also more stable. People were more likely to live in the same district, if not in the same town or village, for generations at a time, and if local records have been preserved there is a good chance of going back three or four generations to about the late 17th century. Unless your family was socially prominent, the chances of going farther are pretty slim. Don't be too disappointed if your lead dries up. You will have placed your ancestors in a certain place and time very different from your own. No less satisfying than the genealogical search is discovering the kind of community from which you stem and being able to add additional foliage to the tree.

Names

An unusual family name is often the spur that sets someone off on the trail of their ancestors. It is usually assumed that an unusual name is easier to trace. Unfortunately, this is often not the case. Family names are the basic clues of the genealogist since they are the first facts you start with, and they may advance your research in unexpected ways. However, family names may also lead to considerable confusion.

Many family connections have been unearthed by simply looking up names in a telephone directory, though again this will not work for a very common name in a particular locality. If the name is unusual, and the place of origin is fairly small, the exercise is worthwhile. Large public libraries usually keep national collections of telephone directories, and very large libraries often have international collections. Alternatively, the consulate of the country concerned can probably help.

Provided the number is not too large, you can circulate the people who share your name in your family's place of origin and, although it is a hit-or-miss kind of procedure, you can count yourself unlucky if you draw a total blank.

Certain names are associated with particular districts, sometimes derived from them, and this is still noticeable in, for example, some Scottish fishing ports. Family names, or surnames, are of comparatively recent origin. In the Middle Ages they did not exist, save as a territorial designation or description of a trade. They came to be more widely adopted because first names were no longer sufficient to identify individuals, and they were acquired in various arbitrary ways. Very often they were bestowed at the whim of a clerk filling in a document. The humorist Moritz Safir once related

U.S. health officers checking steerage (the cheapest accommodation) passengers on a European steamer in 1887. Immigration records may provide evidence of an ancestor's place of origin.

how his grandfather came by the name because, when he went to register, the official happened to observe that he was wearing a large sapphire ring.

Names were also spelled in many different ways, and were often changed, either deliberately or by chance. Many immigrants to North America, particularly from non-English speaking countries, changed their names either to make them easier to pronounce or to disguise their ethnic origins. A story is told of two Irish laborers who settled in Scotland in the 19th century. Their names were O'Dowd and O'Toole, but their sons became known as Doud and Doyle and their grandsons as Dodds and McDouall.

Name changes can often be confirmed by tracking down the relevant deed poll but unless you already suspect a change of name, it will not occur to you to investigate this possibility. Moreover, names may change informally and professional names of writers and actors can throw up further complications.

Groundwork

Practically everyone starts off with some facts, provided by their parents and, with luck, grandparents. You should contact all living relatives, including those remote cousins and seek information from them. It is advisable to present them with all the facts you have collected so far together with a clearly phrased questionnaire. Don't forget to leave space for 'any other information'. Quite probably, some distant cousin will know far more about the family than you do, and they may even possess, for example, the old family Bible which your mother had presumed lost.

Any relatives who still live in the district from which your family originated are particularly useful and you may even be able to enlist them for some on-the-spot research, such as inspecting gravestones or checking local records.

You may find that someone has done most of the work before. However unlikely it seems, a pub-

Wedding photographs tend to be preserved more often than most family documents, and if you know just one member of a group like this you have a good chance of tracking down many of the others. Photographs of a known date can be valuable in revealing the approximate age of individuals.

lished history of your family, or of another family closely connected with it, may exist without your knowledge, and you should confirm that it does not before you get too involved in your own researches. In Britain you may contact the Society of Genealogists or check the British Library catalog for printed family histories. There is a recommended procedure for tracking down other people who may be researching your lines in the United States. First, search the I.G.I. (International Genealogical Index – see page 12), second, contact the genealogical societies in the area concerned (addresses from Mary K. Meyer, *Directory of Genealogical Societies in the USA and Canada*) and also, perhaps, historical societies (addresses in Tracey L. Craig, *Directory of Historical Societies and Agencies in the United States and Canada).* Then try public and university libraries in the area and finally the National Index of Family Associations and Periodicals (3638 Philadelphia Street, Chino, California 91710).

In general, the *National Union Catalog of Manuscript Collections* published by the Library of Congress is the ultimate reference in this area; printed works are naturally easier to track down, through the Library of Congress, the Daughters of the American Revolution Library (also in Washington, D.C.) or major libraries and state historical societies.

Photographs and portraits are very interesting for they can usually be dated fairly accurately, if not by yourself then by an expert in the field, and the clothes or the background may also contain a number of clues. Photographs are often taken on special occasions, and if you can identify the celebration you have a good chance of finding out the date, which may also lead you on to additional sources of data.

Besides all the documentary evidence, valuable sources of information can be discovered among the family possessions. In one case an antique silver teapot provided a valuable clue simply because it was possible to trace the maker, whose records revealed the customer for whom it was made.

However, a word of warning regarding this kind of 'domestic' research: never rely on hearsay alone – at least, not if you are pursuing your ancestral line seriously. If your mother tells you that your grandfather's name was George, she is almost certainly correct. Nevertheless, her word is not proof, for which you will need something like a certified copy of a birth certificate, which may well tell you that in fact your grandfather's first name was Frederick, even though he was universally known to his contemporaries by his second name, George. The custom, which is prevalent in the United States, of naming eldest sons after their father, is not a very helpful one with regard to genealogical research.

If you have never pursued any original historical research before, and not many people have, you should familiarize yourself with general procedures, and the snags you are likely to encounter, before you start. Many colleges and educational institutes now offer courses in family history, and you will spare yourself considerable frustration and bewilderment if you attend one in your area. There are also a number of local and family history societies and organizations like the Daughters of the American Revolution which can provide valuable assistance.

If you prefer, you may turn the whole problem over to a professional genealogist, though this can be very expensive as well as depriving you of the excitement of the chase. There are organizations in

Family mementoes can be informative as well as interesting. Below, a British suffragette medal suggests that great-grandmama was a militant feminist, and (left) a beautiful sampler (demonstrating proficiency in needlework) of 1824 gives details of its nine-year-old maker.

every country which, if you give them a reasonable amount of information to start with, will conduct local investigations for a modest fee, and there may be other areas where you require professional assistance from a professional genealogist. If you do, make sure you do not embark upon an open-ended agreement which may involve you in unforeseen expenses, and avoid agencies which advertize in the press, often promising to discover the coat of arms you are entitled to. Lists of qualified genealogists can be obtained from national and local genealogical societies.

Working Methods

Once you have gained all the information you can from domestic, local and printed sources, you are ready to invade official archives. The basic documents which will confirm the bare facts of the existence of your relatives are records of birth, death, marriage and divorce.

But before you progress any further, organize your system of working. Your records should be clear and accurate, with room to insert new information. Use loose-leaf notebooks, index cards, or a computer. If you are preparing an actual family tree, do not try to include all the biographical details of each individual – just enough to identify him or her. You can compile a more detailed version when your research is complete.

Some people have a natural gift for research, but if you are not one of them, the skill can easily be acquired. It is mainly an attitude of mind and attention to detail. In any kind of historical research, vagueness is fatal and you must know, or be able to find out easily, exactly where a particular piece of information is stored. As your work progresses, you may find that the system you adopted at the beginning is no longer viable. You must, in this case, change the system, but do not simply adapt your method of working as you go along. You may think, 'Oh, I'll remember why I did that', but six months later you probably won't.

The virtues of accuracy and orderliness are especially important when you come to consult old indexes, calendars or documents and reference books. Make sure you understand the system first, and do not go on working after you become tired – or bored. Archives and specialized libraries can be confusing places at first, but they generally work according to some more or less logical system, so make yourself familiar with that first, perhaps by reading a guide published for potential users. If you

do get in a muddle, the staff will probably be sympathetic and helpful, but make yourself as independent of their assistance as you can.

In all forms of research, be on guard against bias, not only the bias present in the document you are consulting, but also your own personal bias. Even in scientific research, it is not uncommon for 'discoveries' to be made because the experiment was designed to fit some preconceived hypothesis. If you are expecting to find a certain fact, you have a natural inclination to find *that* fact and not one that is slightly different. Equally, facts that contradict a hypothesis tend to be overlooked. If for example you are already convinced that a certain person was your great-great-grandfather, your eye will alight eagerly on anything which seems to confirm it and perhaps pass over anything that does not.

Remember too, that newspaper reporters, say, are not on oath! A statement is not necessarily true simply because it appears in print. Moreover, what may be perfectly true in the context, may be open to a different interpretation today. The statement that a certain man was of grossly immoral character may mean something sinister or it may mean that he took a little too much to drink on occasion.

Private documents such as diaries are naturally even more subjective in nature, and allowance must be made for changing attitudes. But few things can be taken absolutely on trust. Even in the computer age, facts are sometimes recorded incorrectly, and this was obviously more common when the record depended on a tired clerk with his quill pen. Mistakes may also be deliberate. It is a time-honored tradition for ladies to be reticent about their age, and census returns are likely to contain many examples of this tendency in action.

Very old handwritten documents are hard to read, and if you are going to do any research among them you will need to have some knowledge of relevant styles. It is not as difficult as it appears at first, since it is largely a matter of growing accustomed to a different set of conventions, such as an S that looks like an F.

Basic Documentation

All births, marriages and deaths are officially recorded, but in most countries this has been done since the 19th century at the earliest, and due to mishaps of one sort or another records are not always complete. In the United States official certificates are filed in the relevant district – there is no Federal record. Copies of birth, death and marriage certificates can be obtained by writing to the appropriate Vital Statistics office of the state or area concerned. There is a small fee, usually not more than $5, and you must give full details in as far as you know them. In the case of birth records this includes: full name, sex and race, parents' names, date of birth, place of birth, purpose of request and relationship to the subject. If you are unable to provide all this data, don't worry. The staff are usually quite dedicated, though they are naturally reluctant to undertake a very prolonged search.

The same kind of rules apply to obtaining such records in other countries. In England and Wales, for example, copies of certificates can be obtained from the General Register Office (G.R.O.) in London. You can conduct your own search in person, but in most circumstances it is easier to do it by post. Even if your search is successful, you cannot obtain a copy of the required certificate on the spot.

In most American states, *full* records do not go much further back than around the turn of the century, but for the earlier period, before vital statistics were registered by the state, they may have been recorded by the county or town. You may encounter unfortunate gaps – Delaware, for example, has birth and death records for 1861-63 but not for 1864-80 – and you may have to look elsewhere for records of, for instance, persons born abroad. Records should be available from the State Department in the case of American citizens who were born or who died in another country.

Naturalization records can also be useful. Copies are normally available from the clerk of the court in which the application was approved, which usually means a federal or state court. Some, up to 1906, are in the National Archives, and some are indexed.

A birth certificate is the basic document to confirm a person's existence, and you should always obtain a certified copy if possible, even when you are already certain of the details.

Censuses

The greatest single source of information about the individual members of a country's population is the census returns. The primary purpose of a census is not to assist genealogists but to compile information about the population which the government needs for administrative purposes. Historically, governments were more interested in property than the individuals, for the purpose of assessing taxes of one sort or another. In this sense the census is an ancient device, one well-known example being the census which resulted in Jesus being born in Bethlehem. A famous medieval European example was the *Domesday Book*, compiled on the orders of William the Conqueror in 1086. The first modern census, which was compiled for political purposes in order to establish who could vote, was the U.S. census of 1790. Although less comprehensive than later censuses, it gave a fair amount of information: the name of the householder, the number of free white males and females, broken down into age groups (0-10 and 10-16), the number of other free persons and of slaves, the county and sometimes the town or district. The 1820 census included non-citizens and a broad occupational breakdown for heads of households. In general, U.S. returns are much more detailed than European equivalents, sometimes even noting physical disabilities.

The mere idea of a census aroused hostility in many places, understandably perhaps given the traditional purpose of such records. Efforts to introduce one in 18th-century Britain were attacked as an infringement of the liberties of the subject. What turned the tide of public opinion was the work of Thomas Malthus, whose theory that population growth would outrun resources suggested the desirability of counting heads. The first census took place in 1801 and, as in the United States, a census has since been conducted every ten years with the exception of 1941.

Since social and political preoccupations vary, so does the type of information in census returns. So far as the family historian is concerned, for instance, the first British census of real use is that of 1841. It listed every person in every household by name, approximate age, sex and occupation, but the returns contain hidden snags, such as the failure to state whether two adult persons, sharing the same family name and being of roughly similar age, are husband and wife or brother and sister. Other snags are common to all census returns, one of the most troublesome being the failure of individuals to tell the truth about themselves.

All U.S. census returns to 1880 are in the National Archives, including its regional branches in Atlanta, Boston, Chicago, Denver, Fort Worth, Kansas City, Los Angeles, Philadelphia, St Louis, San Francisco and Seattle. They may also be inspected on microfiche in many state libraries and the offices of historical societies. For state censuses, consult the guide by Henry J. Dubester, published by the Federal government, *State Censuses, An Annotated Bibliography . . .*

English and Welsh census returns are in the Public Record Office (P.R.O.) in London, and most of them are now available on microfiche. Scottish census returns are at New Register House in Edinburgh, Irish in the Dublin P.R.O. (the Irish records are severely depleted as a result of a disastrous fire in 1922). Canadian census returns date from 1851 but are incomplete before 1871. Foreign consulates will direct you to the source of census returns in their countries.

Searching census returns, which are not (or not necessarily) arranged alphabetically by families, can be a bore if there is no index and you do not know the exact address, and the microfiche scanners take a little getting used to. If you are faced with searching a large area, it sometimes pays to attempt to discover the address first from some other source, such as trade directories, in the local library. If that does not produce results, you will probably have to undertake the job yourself (or by hired proxy) since even the most helpful staff cannot be expected to wade through every household in a given town. Luckily, an increasing number of census returns nowadays do have printed indexes, though of course this does not obviate the need to consult the returns themselves.

Church Records

With luck, records of births, marriages and deaths, plus the census returns, will take you back to the beginning of the 19th century, but civil records, even if they take you that far, will not take you much farther. Church records can often provide a useful alternative.

There are a number of published guides to Church records in the United States, and you may obtain access to the records either through individual churches or through the central archives of the relevant body. State and local libraries and historical societies can provide guidance. The ultimate source in England is the *National Index of Parish Registers*, although County Record Offices usually have the necessary information. English parish registers are concerned only with members of the Church of England and, even when that was supposed to include the whole population, it did not. The records of other Churches and religious bodies are very variable in quality. Famous for their comprehensiveness are the records of births, marriages and deaths kept by the Society of Friends (the Quakers) since the middle of the 17th century.

An important point to remember with Church records is that the events registered are not births, marriages and deaths, but baptisms (in Christian churches), marriages and burials. Normally, there is not much difference between the date of death and the date of burial, but that is not always so and, in the case of birth and baptism, there may well be a long delay. Moreover, there is usually no way to tell whether such a gap has occurred; most Church records do not give actual birth and death dates.

Those pursuing British ancestors to a relatively remote era are fortunate in that parish registers have been remarkably well preserved. In England

and Wales they date back to 1538, when the keeping of such registers was made compulsory, and there are a few from even earlier times. Scottish registers date from 1558, Irish from 1634. Naturally, there are gaps, in even the best preserved records, particularly during the political turmoil of the mid-17th century; otherwise, the situation varies from parish to parish. Some records have disappeared entirely, but in general there is a good chance of finding the registers back to about 1660. Check with the County Record Office, where you may find the register you want has actually been printed – a special advantage if you are not at ease with 17th-century handwriting – or ask the priest of the parish concerned. There is normally a small fee, and it is tactful, since parish priests are not well paid, to enclose an International Reply Coupon.

Do make sure you have the right parish. The parish you are concerned with may no longer exist, and if it does, its boundaries may well have changed at least once over the years.

The problem of territorial boundaries in general, though always soluble, can be considerable. The justly unpopular reorganization of local government in England in 1974, which altered many old county boundaries, is just one recent example of the trouble administrators make for family historians. There are larger problems than that, however. The American genealogist George B. Everton, Sr, quotes an example of a man who was known to have died in 1869 in Ford County, Illinois, at the age of 75, and to have lived in the same district all his life. The records for Ford County would have been of limited help in this case, because it was only formed in 1859, from Clark County. However, Clark County only dated from 1819, when it was formed from Crawford County, which in turn was formed from Edwards County in 1816. The latter was but a short-lived entity, having been created out of Madison and Gallatin Counties two years earlier. Madison County (formed 1812) descended from St Clair County (1790), and Gallatin from Randolph County (1795), the latter being another, older, formation from St Clair County.

Once you have tracked your ancestor to a particular parish, a personal visit, if possible, has many advantages. Not only do you soak up some of the atmosphere and perhaps learn interesting details from the current residents, but you may also find other direct evidence, such as a tombstone. Unfortunately, inscriptions on tombstones tend to grow illegible in time. They are now being recorded, by family history societies among others, while many American states have card indexes for tombstones. Occasionally they were recorded some time ago. In

Gravestones, like these in Lenox, MA, may provide a bonus, as they often survive accidents which destroy paper records; they also usually give death date (not burial date).

the English county of Gloucestershire, for example, most graveyard inscriptions were written down in the 1780s, with the result that 16th-17th century inscriptions which would otherwise have vanished long ago have been preserved.

Besides the registers, there are other church documents which may provide relevant data. For example, after the introduction of the Elizabethan Poor Law in England, Overseers of the Poor in each parish had to keep a record of their accounts. Here is one area where someone who had the misfortune to be a pauper is more easily found than someone of greater prosperity!

The International Genealogical Index (I.G.I.)

All modern genealogists acknowledge a great debt to the Church of Latter-Day Saints of Jesus Christ, more familiarly known as the Mormons. Their library in Salt Lake City is probably the largest repository of international genealogical information in the world. It contains all kinds of relevant records from about 40 countries, in particular a constantly expanding index of parish records covering the period from 1538 to the 19th century. The motive for this remarkable record is the Mormons' dedication to retrospective baptism of their ancestors by proxy. The record is therefore primarily of baptisms,

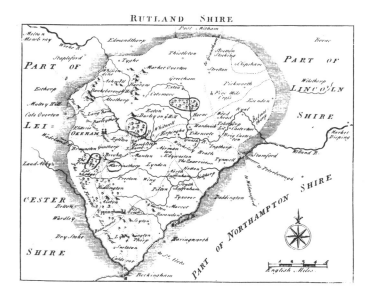

Old maps are an invaluable source for local history. This one shows the former English county of Rutland which was amalgamated with Leicestershire in 1974.

although some marriages are included, but it represents an invaluable short cut when searching for parish records. It is, however, what it says it is – an index – and the records themselves, having been located through the I.G.I., must then be consulted. Besides Salt Lake City, the microfiched index can be consulted in Mormon libraries throughout the world as well as in certain other institutions, such as the Society of Genealogists Library in London. Local record offices have microfiches of their own district.

Wills

A will is of obvious interest if you can find it as, unlike the official documents mentioned above, it is personal, and is the actual 'testament' of the person who made it. It is often the only direct testament you have of the person concerned, and you may find it contains a good deal of unexpected information which will provide a fuller picture of your ancestor's life than any other formal document is likely to do. In your research so far you will, for the most part, have been recovering facts of a broadly predictable kind, from fairly obvious sources. Wills are different: they are often less easily found and their value varies enormously, but until you have seen them you cannot tell how much help, if any, they will be.

A will tells you when a person died (you will usually know this already) and what their material circumstances were. With luck it will tell you a lot more: what his (it is more often a man, especially as you go farther back in time, for obvious reasons) occupation was and what sort of life he lived. Sometimes other documents are attached, such as an inventory of the possessions of the deceased, which can be of great interest. A will can suddenly bring your ancestor much closer, making him into a flesh and blood figure instead of just a name and some dates. Wills may be humorous, pathetic or malignant, and may contain bequests that are now impossible to understand. Sometimes they may solve longstanding family mysteries.

A great many wills are recorded on film in the Mormons' library, and that is the first place to check. Otherwise you have to approach the clerk of the relevant probate court. In England and Wales, all wills since 1858 were proved in the Principal Probate Registry at Somerset House or at a District Probate Registry (in which case they are indexed at Somerset House).

With wills, as with other records, the farther you

A will may be the only direct, personal evidence you have of an ancestor. In earlier times a woman's property passed to her husband on marriage, and therefore old wills are more often by men than women.

go back in time, the more difficult the search becomes, and this is an area in which you may well decide to seek professional advice. A trained genealogist who is familiar with the field will certainly complete the search more quickly than an amateur, but in the majority of cases, if the will exists it will be in some central repository. Local family history societies can usually indicate the likely place, and you may even find that the will you are looking for has been printed.

There are a number of factors which can complicate the search for a will. Sometimes a long period elapsed before the will was proved, and if you are unable to locate it in the year of the person's death that does not mean the will is absent. Also, wills are not always proved in the obvious probate court. For example, if the executors lived in another part of the country they may have found it more convenient to have the will proved in their own district. Finally, a minor point: some wills can be excessively long, and before you order a photocopy of the document it is advisable to find out just how long it is!

Printed Works

Apart from the types of printed sources mentioned earlier, your investigation of your family history is certain to involve you in some more general reading. If, for example, you discover that you are descended from someone who fought in the American, or even English, Civil War, you will want to learn more about that conflict, especially campaigns or other aspects of it in which your ancestor was involved. The chances are that if you are sufficiently interested in the past to seek out your ancestors, you have some background knowledge of history anyway, but you will not know all about soldiering under General Grant or General Lee, or under Oliver Cromwell or Prince Rupert. If you are comparatively ignorant of the historical situation, you are likely to miss the full significance of the facts you discover. Although some people pass their lives untouched by the large events of history, the behaviour of individuals is inevitably shaped to some extent by contemporary conditions.

Besides general background material, books and other printed documents may give you some direct facts about your ancestors. Most of the more common examples have already been mentioned, but the reference library contains a great variety of works which may be of further use.

The most obvious are biographical dictionaries. If your ancestor was an eminent person, you may find him or her in a dictionary of national biography. If you have discovered a link with the English nobility, suspicion (or fond hope) of which is a frequent motive for genealogical searches, you are in clover: it is an easy matter to follow the line back to the creation of the title (sometimes, of course, this is not so far as people are inclined to suppose) through such a work as *Burke's Peerage* or, if there were estates but no title, *Burke's Landed Gentry*. One point to remember with such works is that the latest edition is not necessarily the best, from your point of view; earlier editions may give more detail. For example, the second edition of *Burke's Landed Gentry*, published in 1840-1849, runs to three volumes and has an index over 300 pages long. More recent figures of some attainment may be found in the relevant national *Who's Who*.

Persons of less fame may be found in the astonishing number and variety of biographical dictionaries devoted to a particular trade or profession, in a particular era. If, to take a random example, your ancestor was an early New England clockmaker, you can be virtually certain that his life has been researched and the results published in

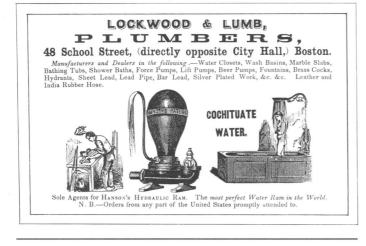

LOCKWOOD & LUMB,
P L U M B E R S,
48 School Street, (directly opposite City Hall,) Boston.

Manufacturers and Dealers in the following.—Water Closets, Wash Basins, Marble Slabs, Bathing Tubs, Shower Baths, Force Pumps, Lift Pumps, Beer Pumps, Fountains, Brass Cocks, Hydrants, Sheet Lead, Lead Pipe, Bar Lead, Silver Plated Work, &c. &c. Leather and India Rubber Hose.

COCHITUATE WATER.

Sole Agents for HANSON'S HYDRAULIC RAM. The *most perfect Water Ram in the World.*
N. B.—Orders from any part of the United States promptly attended to.

Commercial announcements, advertisements and trade cards may provide information not obtainable elsewhere, such as address or occupation, and may lead to further sources.

probably more than one book (though, it must be admitted, they may be rather meagre). Some fields of work are, naturally, better covered than others. The arts and crafts tend to be particularly well served (someone so humble as a silhouette cutter in a Victorian seaside town has probably been the subject of some eager student's research), but the professions are also well catered for, especially the military. For other crafts and vocations, if there is no relevant biographical dictionary, there may be histories of the trade concerned.

Directories are another useful category. They go back a surprisingly long way: the first London directory was published over 300 years ago, and most large towns had directories of their own by about 1800. The early ones, though mainly confined to tradespeople and officials, often include private citizens as well, and they give a general picture of the town, with details on local industries, education, transport, etc. Old directories can be useful in locating addresses, but there are some snags here because the adoption of fixed addresses is only about as old as the national postal system, and previously they tended to be inaccurate. Even after house numbers became standard, no great reliance can be placed on them as they appear in an old directory, because they have probably changed. So have streets and street names, and you will need to consult a contemporary map to pin down a precise location. Sometimes it appears that a family moved house, because the number or street has changed, but this may simply mean that the street was renumbered or its name changed. Another point to keep in mind is that the information in directories

is generally about a year out of date – that much time at least having elapsed between compilation of data and publication. This may explain such anomalies as a different address being given in the census and a directory of the same year.

Old newspapers and periodicals are a source of many kinds of information, but before you venture upon this ocean of newsprint, you need to consult an index. Some major newspapers such as the *New York Times* and *The Times* of London are indexed, but most are not, and in that case you will need to have a good idea of the date on which the item you are looking for appeared. Very often, as in an obituary for instance, you should not have to search through more than a few days. For periodicals, you first need a retrospective index of publications, which is available in any large reference library, but whether there is an index of the actual periodical in which you are interested is another matter. Many journals have an annual index, published in a particular issue, but in earlier times this is less common. There are various other indexes of obituaries etc. published by antiquarian societies, but even if you have the patience of Job, there is little point in wading through several years' run of, say, *The Stockbreeder's Gazette*, on the offchance of finding an item relevant to your research. The use of old magazines of a certain kind (such as *The Gentleman's Magazine*, first published in 1731) for straight genealogical research has become largely redundant thanks to the I.G.I., but remember that there may well be extra details (e.g. names of guests at a wedding) in the old publications.

Among other reference books, encyclopedias (especially topical ones), historical atlases and gazetteers should be mentioned. Their usefulness is obvious enough. Back copies of annual reference publications should not be ignored. The *Editor and Publisher's Market Guide* is a modern example, and the back issues provide a wealth of interesting information for social historians. As Jacques Barzun remarked (in *The Modern Researcher*, a book still well worth reading though first published over thirty years ago), it tells you 'how many drugstores there are in Atlanta, the resources of the banks in Spokane, and the quality of the tap water in Cheyenne.'

Inevitably, there will be times when you find yourself in the frustrating situation of not knowing exactly what you are looking for and undecided about where you should begin. Fortunately, most librarians are very helpful people and there are a host of professional people, besides well-informed amateurs, whom you can call upon for help. Sometimes they become as involved in the quest as you are so do not be afraid to ask for advice, detailing exactly what you hope to find out.

Immigration

If you are a U.S. citizen, or a Canadian, an Australian, etc., and unless you belong to the aboriginal populations of those countries, your search for your ancestors is probably going to take you to another – most often European – country. This obviously poses certain problems, but it also has at least one advantage. Records were kept of both emigrants and immigrants, and although they are patchy, if you cannot find a record of your ancestor's immigration, you may find him or her recorded as an emigrant in the country of origin.

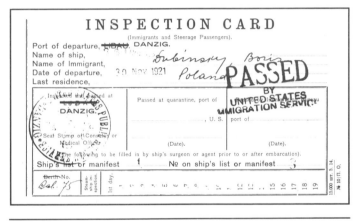

The collection of immigration data began in 1820, though unfortunately the records are not complete. In the all-important matter of origin, the country is usually given but the district less often.

If the person concerned was of some contemporary prominence, you should have little trouble in locating their movements. In fact they may have been traced already. We know more about the antecedents of George Washington, for example, than he knew himself (though this is not, as it happens, a great deal). If your ancestors were not people of any note, the task becomes harder, especially if immigration occurred more than about 100 years ago. In that case, if you do not know the date of immigration, nor the immigrant's place of origin, you are in serious difficulties, especially if the family name was a common one.

Place of origin is the crucial factor. If you know that, you are at least on the same footing with people whose ancestors never left the country. The place can often be discovered from death certifi-

cates, naturalization papers and other records, but without it, you face formidable problems.

Printed sources may, again, come to your aid. Much work has been done on the early settlers in America in particular, and there are published lists of immigrants as well as bibliographies of ships' passenger lists. These are obviously the first place to look, provided you know the approximate date of emigration, but unfortunately the records are far from comprehensive and, if you are lucky enough to find your ancestor listed, the place of origin may not be given, in which case you have not advanced very much further. In Britain, passenger lists were kept on a regular basis only from 1890; earlier, the gaps widen. On the immigrant side, comprehensive records go back to about the same time (when the immigration bureau was established on Ellis Island in 1892). Lists of passengers arriving in U.S. ports from about 1835 exist in the National Archives, but they are not complete and do not give exact places of origin. For the earlier period, throughout the 18th century, records are sparse. British Customs officials kept returns of emigrants leaving British ports, but they perished in a fire in 1814.

If you are seeking ancestors of British origin and you do not know the date of emigration or place of origin, there are still other avenues to explore. If the family name was very uncommon, you may be able to trace it to a particular district with the help of such a reference work as *Homes of Family Names in Great Britain* (1890), by H. B. Guppy. You may discover a relative's will through the printed index. In the case of a very early immigrant, before about 1630, the royal license to emigrate may be recorded.

If the immigrant arrived in North America as an indentured servant, there must have been a written contract. If this can be found, it provides invaluable information. Some of these indentures are held among the Treasury papers in the Public Record Office, and there is an (incomplete) index by name. Alternatively, you may find it easier to track down the man's master, who will give you a fairly, if not completely, reliable guide to the place of origin.

Death certificates of American immigrants sometimes mention length of residence, from which you can deduce date of emigration. Additionally, colonial immigrants sometimes received land grants from the British Crown, and there are indexes of these, plus copies of the actual documents, in the Library of Congress.

In short, there is nearly always some course to follow, although the prospects may not look promising and the time may come when you have to acknowledge defeat. Meanwhile, much depends on the strength of your determination.

Some Useful Addresses

AUSTRALIA

Australian Society of Genealogy, Richmond Villa, 120 Kent Street, Sydney, N.S.W. 2000

Australian Society of Genealogy Studies, P.O. Box 68, Oakleigh, Vic. 3166

Genealogical Society of Tasmania, P.O. Box 6400, Hobart, Tas. 7001

Genealogy Society of Queensland, P.O. Box 423, Woolloongabba, Qld. 4012

Genealogy Society of the Northern Territory, P.O. Box 37212, Winnellie, N.T. 0789

Genealogy Society of Victoria, 5th Floor, Curtin House, 252 Swanston Street, Melbourne, Vic. 3000

Heraldry and Genealogy Society of Canberra, G.P.O. Box 585, Canberra, A.C.T. 2601

Queensland Family History Society, P.O. Box 171, Indrooopilly, Qld. 4068

The South Australian Genealogy and Heraldry Society Incorporated, G.P.O. Box 592, Adelaide, S.A. 5001

Western Australia Genealogy Society, Unit 5, 48 May Street, Bayswater, W.A. 6053

BRITISH ISLES

Association of Genealogists and Record Agents, 1 Woodside Close, Caterham, Surrey

(Church of Jesus Christ of Latter-Day Saints) Family History Library, 64-68 Exhibition Road, London S.W.7

Federation of Family History Societies, 96 Beaumont Street, Milehouse, Plymouth, Devon PL2 3AQ

General Register Office (England and Wales), St Catherine's House, 10 Kingsway, London WC2B 6JB; (Scotland) New Register House, Edinburgh EH1 3YT; (Northern Ireland) 49-55 Chichester Street, Belfast BT1 4HL; (Republic of Ireland) Joyce House, 8-11 Lombard Street E., Dublin 2

Public Record Office (England and Wales), Chancery Lane, London WC2A 1LR; (Census) Portugal Street, London WC2A 3PH; (most government departmental records) Ruskin Avenue, Kew, Richmond, Surrey TW9 4DU; Scottish Record Office, New Register House, Edinburgh EH1 3YT; (Northern Ireland), 66 Balmoral Avenue, Belfast BT9 6NY; (Republic of Ireland), Four Courts, The Castle, Dublin 7

Scottish Genealogical Society, 9 Union Street, Edinburgh

Society of Genealogists, 14 Charterhouse Buildings, London E.C.1

NEW ZEALAND

Alexander Turnbull Library, c/o National Library of New Zealand, P.O. Box 12349, Wellington

Family History Centre, c/o Mr W. D. Cummings, 9 McKay Drive, Templeview, Hamilton

The Genealogy Library, Auckland Institute and Museum, Private Bag, Auckland

New Zealand and Pacific Department, c/o The Librarian, P.O. Box 4138, Auckland

New Zealand Society of Genealogists, P.O. Box 8795, Auckland

SOUTH AFRICA

Genealogical Society of South Africa, P.O. Box 4839, Cape Town 8000

UNITED STATES OF AMERICA

American Society of Genealogists, 1228 Eye Street N.W., Washington, D.C. 20005

Board for the Certification of Genealogists, 1307 New Hampshire Avenue N.E., Washington, D.C.

Church of Jesus Christ of Latter-Day Saints, 50 E. North Temple Street, Salt Lake City, Utah 84150

Library of Congress, Washington, D.C. 20540

National Archives, Pennsylvania Avenue, Washington, D.C. 20408

National Genealogical Society, 1921 Sunderland Place N.W., Washington, D.C. 20005

Some Useful Books

American Association for State and Local History, *Directory, Historical Societies and Agencies in the United States and Canada* 12th ed. 1982

C.E. Banks and E.E. Brownell, *Topographical Dictionary of 2,885 English Emigrants to New England, 1620-50* 1974

Donald R. Barnes and Richard S. Lackey, *Write it Right: A Manual for Writing Family Histories and Genealogies* 1983

A.J. Camp, *Wills and their Whereabouts* (U.K.) 1974

B.R. Crick and M. Alman, *Guide to Manuscripts Relating to America in Great Britain and Ireland* 1961

Noel Currier-Briggs, *Worldwide Family History* 1982

Gilbert H. Doane, *Searching for Your Ancestors,* 1973

Arlene Eakle and Johni Cerni (eds) *The Source: A Guidebook of American Genealogy* 1984

G. Emmison, *Archives and Local History* (in U.K.) 1974

George B. Everton, Sr (ed.), *The Handy Book for Genealogists,* 7th ed. 1981

Val D. Greenwood, *The Researcher's Guide to American Genealogy* 1973

Guide to Genealogical Research in the National Archives 1982

Gerald Hamilton-Edwards, *In Search of Scottish Ancestry* 1972

N.T. Hansen, *Guide to Genealogical Sources – Australia and New Zealand* 1963

HMSO, *British National Archives* 1980

HMSO, *Guide to the Contents of the Public Record Office,* 3 vols, 1963-69

Marion J. Kaminkow, *A New Bibliography of British Genealogy* 1965

Marion J. Kaminkow, *Genealogical Manuscripts and British Libraries* 1967

Marion J. Kaminkow, *Genealogies in the Library of Congress: A Bibliography* 1972

Marion J. Kaminkow, *U.S. Local Histories in the Library of Congress: A Bibliography* 1975-76

E.K. Kirkham, *A Survey of American Census Schedules* 1961

New York Public Library, *Research Libraries: Dictionary Catalog of the Local History and Genealogy Division* 1971

H. Lancour and R.J. Wolfe, *Bibliography of Ship Passenger Lists 1538-1825,* 1969

Allan J. Lichtman, *Your Family History* 1978

Public Archives of Canada, *Tracing Your Ancestors in Canada* 1972

Royal Ministry for Foreign Affairs (Swedish), *Finding Your Forefathers: Some Hints for Americans of Swedish Origin* 1976

C.N. and A.P.S. Smith, *Encyclopedia of German-American Genealogical Research* 1976

F. Smith and D.E. Gardner, *Genealogical Research in England and Wales,* 3 vols, 1956-64

Noel C. Stevenson, *Genealogical Evidence,* 1979

D. Whyte, *Introducing Scottish Genealogical Research* 1979

A.J. Willis, *Genealogy for Beginners* 1979

Governments and genealogical organizations publish many leaflets and guides to researching family history. For example, guides to locating vital records published by the Public Health Service can be obtained from the Superintendent of Documents, U.S. Government Printing Office, Washington, D.C. 20402. A guide to *Tracing Immigrant Ancestors* is published by the Genealogical Institute. There are also many periodicals, such as *Family Tree* in England, or *The Genealogical Helper* in the United States. Many state or local societies have their own periodicals.

The coat of arms adopted by Christopher Columbus in 1502. Arms frequently display symbols appropriate to the activities of their bearers.

THIS FAMILY HISTORY
was researched and compiled by

Name ....

Place ....

Date ....

*This section is designed for you to embellish with your very own family records.
Fill in the details of your genealogical tree and use the key headings to set out information,
photographs and documents you have gathered pertaining to you, your immediate family
and your forebears.*

CONTENTS

OUR FAMILY TREE

HUSBAND'S FULL NAME

WIFE'S FULL NAME

DATE OF MARRIAGE   PLACE OF MARRIAGE

CHILDREN

Family Tree

_____

HUSBAND'S PATERNAL GRANDFATHER'S FULL NAME
_____

HUSBAND'S PATERNAL GRANDMOTHER'S FULL NAME
_____

DATE OF MARRIAGE   PLACE OF MARRIAGE
_____

CHILDREN
_____
_____
_____

_____
HUSBAND'S FATHER'S FULL NAME
_____

HUSBAND'S MOTHER'S FULL NAME
_____

DATE OF MARRIAGE   PLACE OF MARRIAGE
_____

CHILDREN
_____
_____

_____

HUSBAND'S MATERNAL GRANDFATHER'S FULL NAME
_____

HUSBAND'S MATERNAL GRANDMOTHER'S FULL NAME
_____

DATE OF MARRIAGE   PLACE OF MARRIAGE
_____

CHILDREN
_____
_____

_____

WIFE'S PATERNAL GRANDFATHER'S FULL NAME
_____

WIFE'S PATERNAL GRANDMOTHER'S FULL NAME
_____

DATE OF MARRIAGE   PLACE OF MARRIAGE
_____

CHILDREN
_____
_____

_____

_____
WIFE'S FATHER'S FULL NAME
_____

WIFE'S MOTHER'S FULL NAME
_____

DATE OF MARRIAGE   PLACE OF MARRIAGE
_____

CHILDREN
_____
_____

_____

_____

WIFE'S MATERNAL GRANDFATHER'S FULL NAME
_____

WIFE'S MATERNAL GRANDMOTHER'S FULL NAME
_____

DATE OF MARRIAGE   PLACE OF MARRIAGE
_____

CHILDREN
_____
_____

HUSBAND

Husband's full name

Place of birth

Date of birth

WIFE

Wife's full name

Place of birth

Date of birth

CHILDREN

Full name	Place of birth	Date of birth

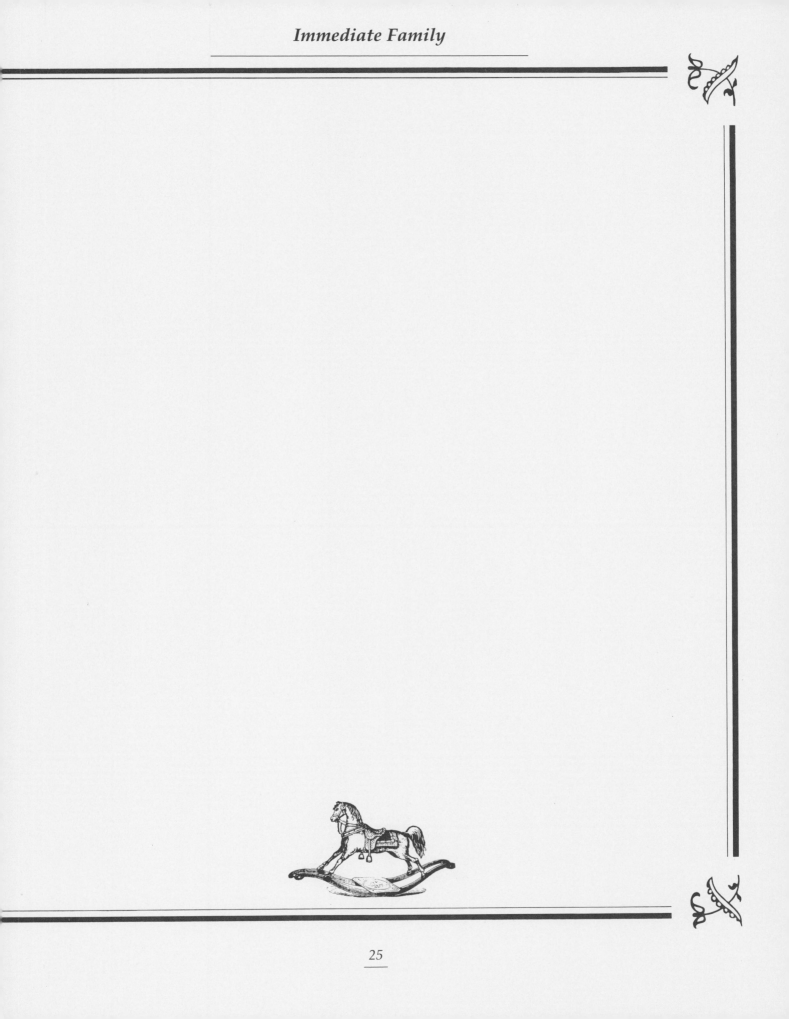

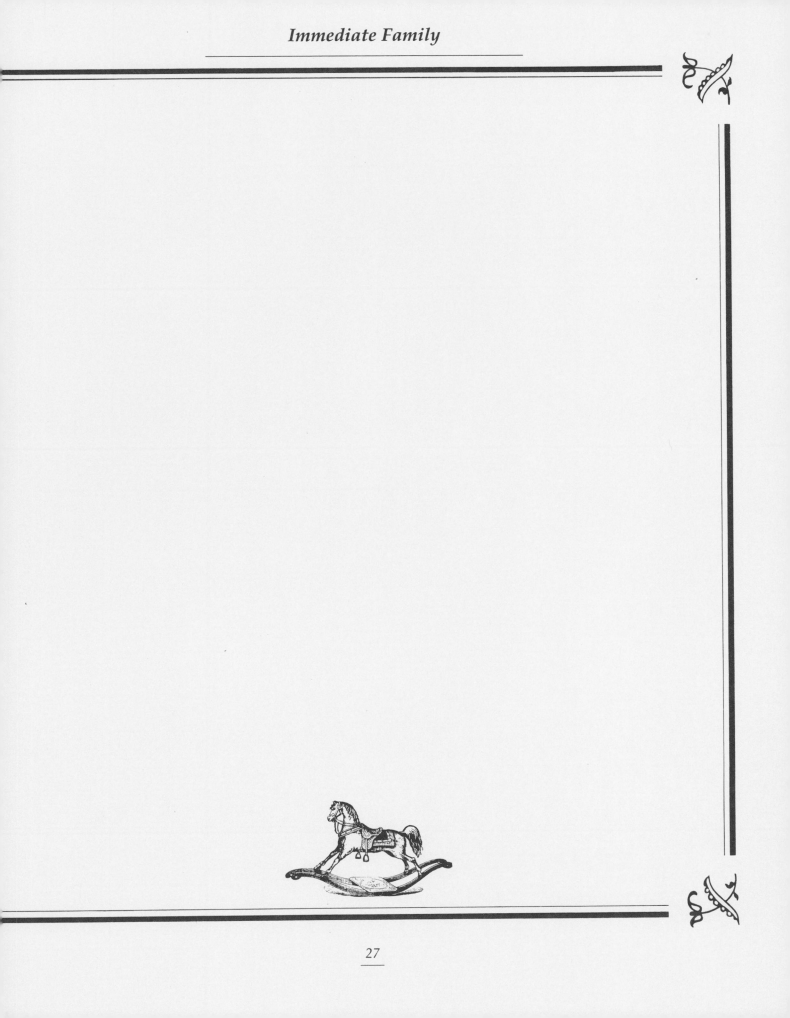

GRANDCHILDREN

Full name	Place of birth	Date of birth

HUSBAND'S PARENTS
(and their children)

Husband's father's full name

Place of birth

Date of birth

Husband's mother's full name

Place of birth

Date of birth

HUSBAND'S PATERNAL GRANDPARENTS
(and their children)

Husband's paternal grandfather's full name

Place of birth

Date of birth

Husband's paternal grandmother's full name

Place of birth

Date of birth

HUSBAND'S MATERNAL GRANDPARENTS
(and their children)

Husband's maternal grandfather's full name

Place of birth

Date of birth

Husband's maternal grandmother's full name

Place of birth

Date of birth

HUSBAND'S EARLY ANCESTORS

WIFE'S PARENTS
(and their children)

Wife's father's full name

Place of birth

Date of birth

Wife's mother's full name

Place of birth

Date of birth

WIFE'S PATERNAL GRANDPARENTS
(and their children)

Wife's paternal grandfather's full name

Place of birth

Date of birth

Wife's paternal grandmother's full name

Place of birth

Date of birth

WIFE'S MATERNAL GRANDPARENTS
(and their children)

Wife's maternal grandfather's full name

Place of birth

Date of birth

Wife's maternal grandmother's full name

Place of birth

Date of birth

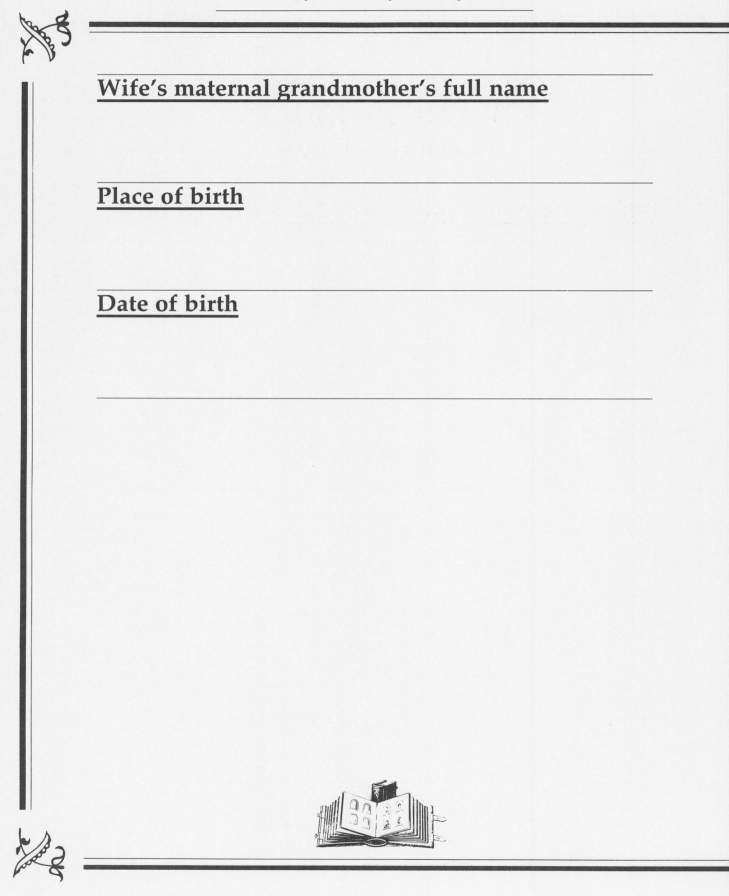

WIFE'S EARLY ANCESTORS

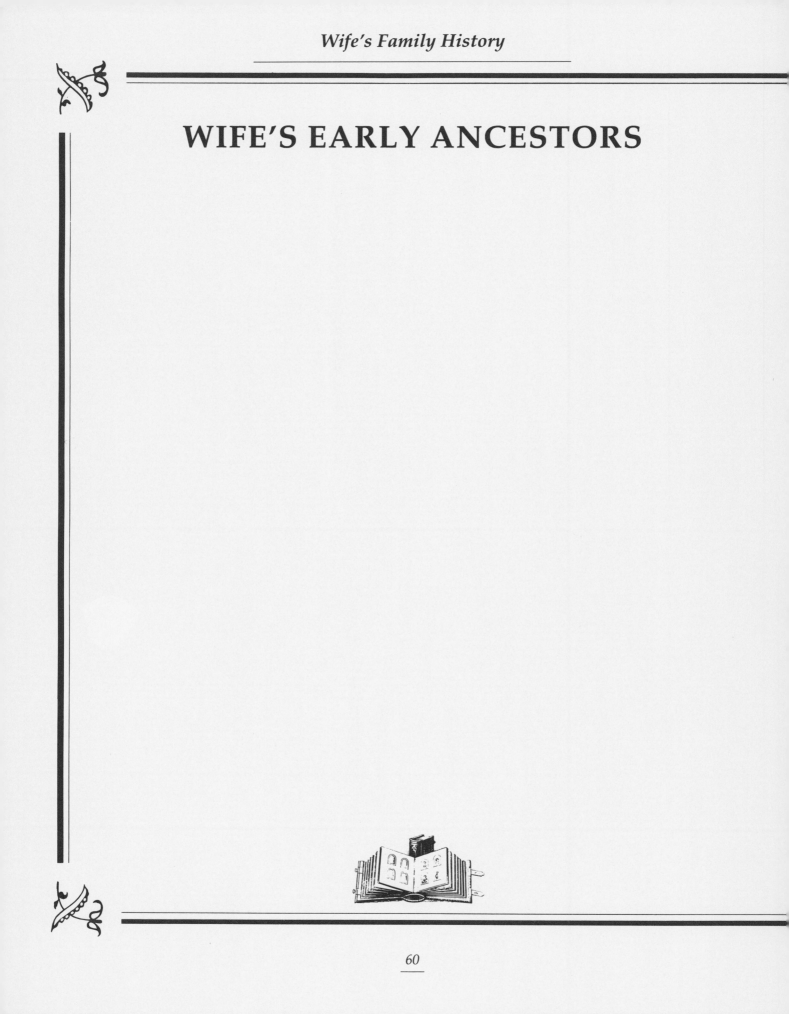

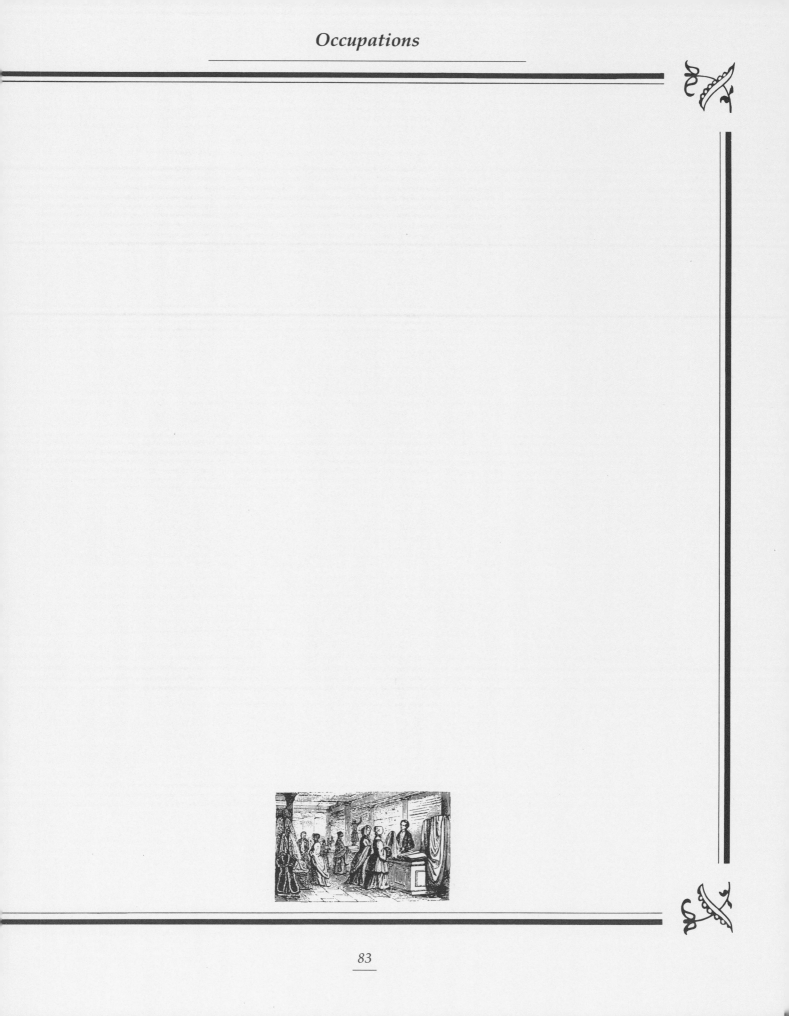

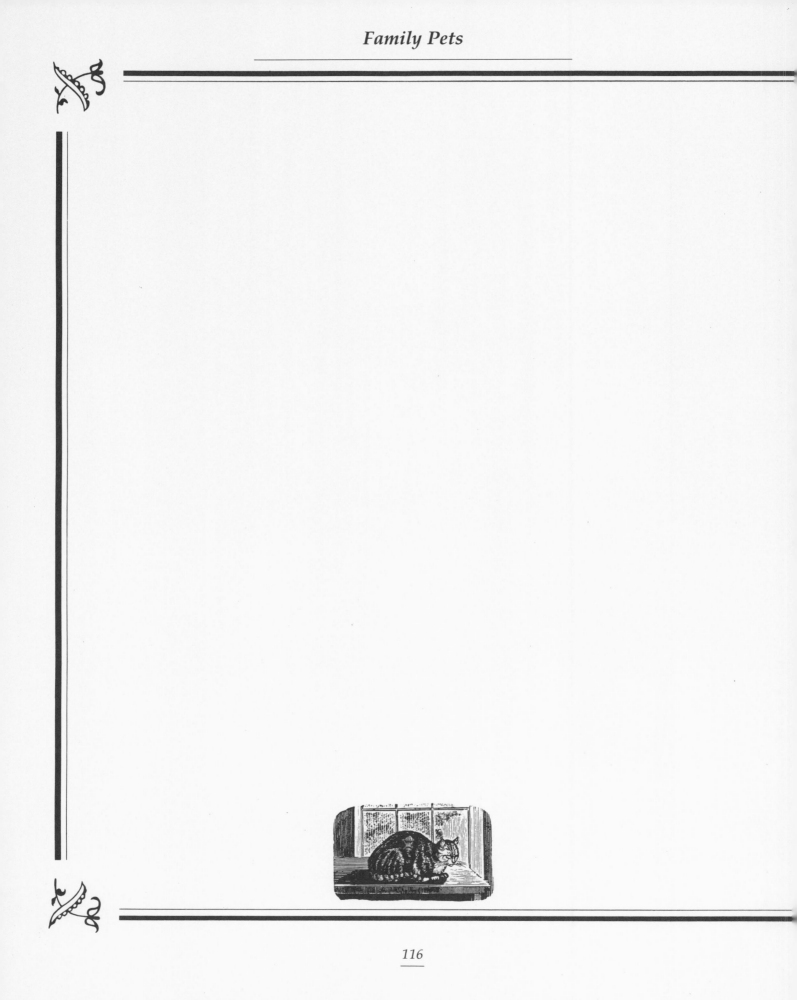